Living with Passion

An Inspirational Guide for Life

Karen Putz

www.agelesspassions.com

This book is dedicated
to
Diane Brogan

"You can do it if you try."

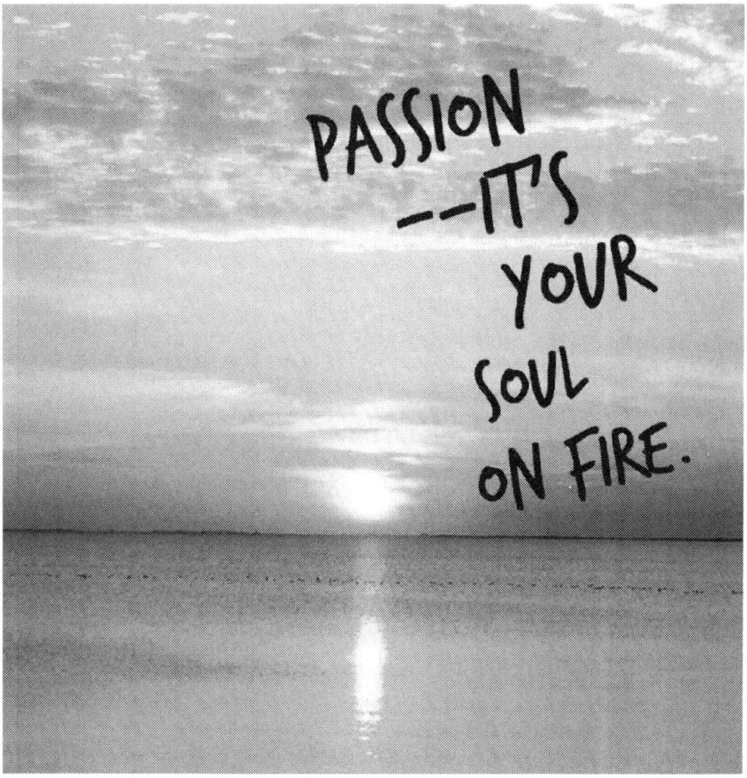
PASSION
--IT'S
YOUR
SOUL
ON FIRE.

The most powerful thing is the human soul on fire, says Ferdinand Foch.

As a Passion Mentor, I frequently have people tell me,

"I don't know what my passion is."

Trust me, you know.

You did not get through this life without experiencing moments of passion—whether it's an interest in something that fascinates you, a feeling of joy, a knowing of what you like and don't like—there's all different dimensions of what we know as passion.

Maybe you became a "grown up" and simply lost your way among the routine of life.

Maybe you just forgot.

As Ben Franklin said, "Some men die at 25 but aren't buried until 75."

Check your pulse—it's still there, isn't it? So you have the capacity to create a life centered around what really matters to you.

Let's begin.

TO SEE A WORLD IN
A GRAIN OF SAND,
AND A HEAVEN IN
A WILD FLOWER,
HOLD INFINITY IN THE PALM
OF YOUR HAND,
AND ETERNITY IN AN HOUR...
—WILLIAM BLAKE

Today's a great day to revisit the moments in your life when you felt those feelings of joy and excitement.

What were you doing?

Who were you with?

Where were you at?

Our past often has the clues we need to determine what kind of life we want to live.

There's a big, huge, beautiful world out there.

And there's only one you.

You were born beautifully unique with a combination of talents, skills, abilities, and interests that no one else has.

No other human being in the world is exactly like you...

"Whenever you are faced with a decision, a choice, or an opportunity, always choose in favor of your passions."

~Janet and Chris Attwood, The Passion Test

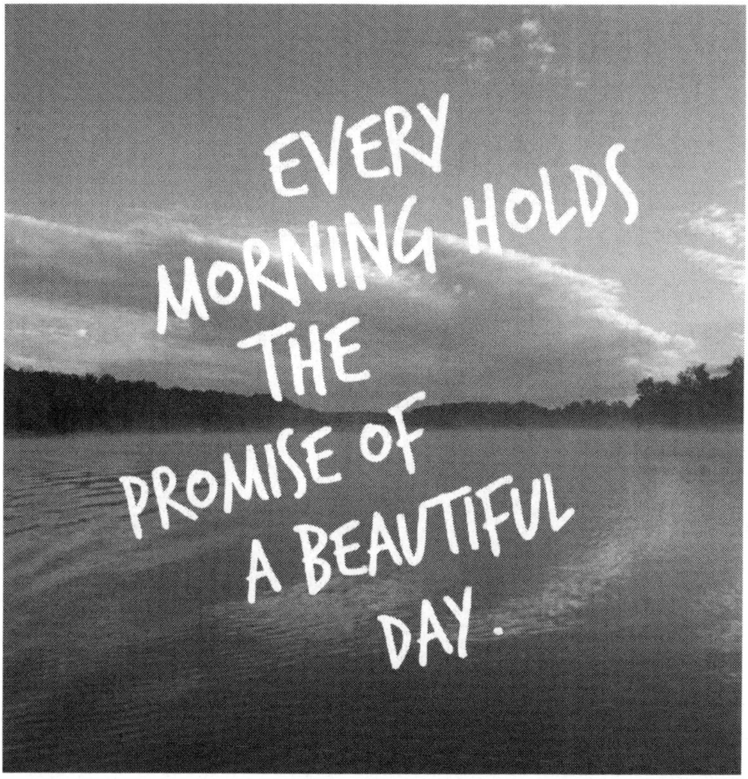
EVERY
MORNING HOLDS
THE
PROMISE OF
A BEAUTIFUL
DAY.

We are on this earth for a very short time. We were not meant to live in misery from day to day. Joy is a beautiful thing to experience and to know.

Every morning that you wake up—you're given the gift of another day. Every morning holds the promise of a beautiful day.

Begin with the practice of gratitude.

What are you grateful for?

Go forth in your day and find the beauty within every moment.

So you have a **dream.**

Yet, it's been nothing but challenges, struggles, and frustration.

How much do you want it?

How passionate are you?

How much do you truly believe in your dream?

Persist.

Change, grow, test, revise, re-do.

If you give up, you'll never know how close you are.

Breakthroughs happen with persistence.

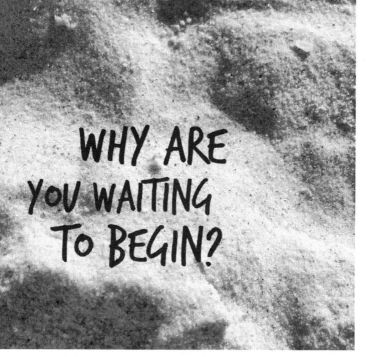

Do you have "Someday Syndrome?"

You know the one.

Someday I'm going to go to Hawaii.

Someday I'm going to write a book.

Someday I'm going to try that new recipe.

Someday I'm going to take a dance class.

Someday I'm going to do that winery tour.

Someday I'm going to...

You can search the world all over and

you will not find a "Someday" on a calendar anywhere.

And the biggest problem of waiting for "Someday..."

You might run out of time.

Begin now.

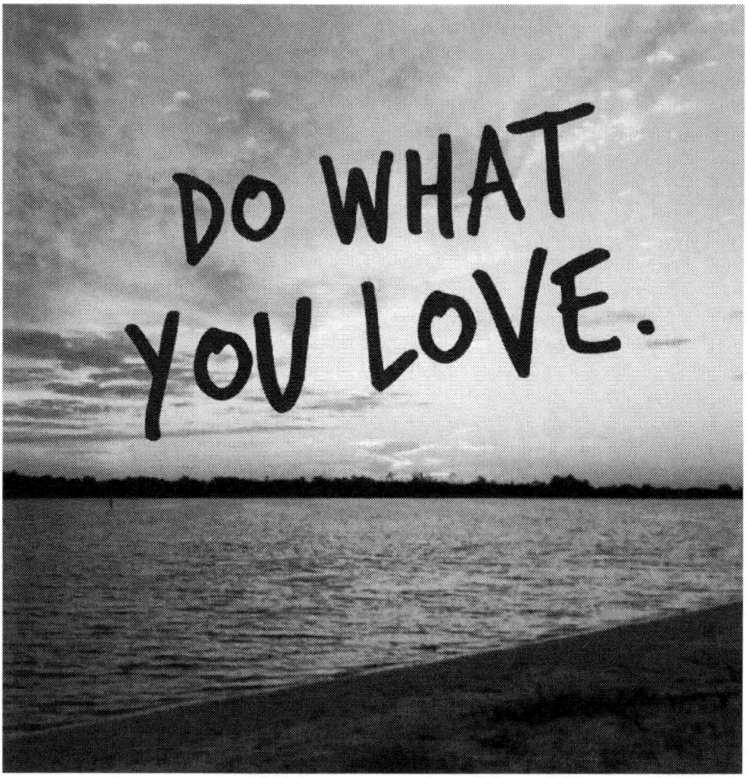
DO WHAT
YOU LOVE.

When you are engaged in something you truly love to do, time fades into the background. The most passionate, happy, joyful people I know are operating from a place of love and service.

Do what you love.

Love what you do.

"The master in the art of living makes little distinction between his work and his play, his labor and his leisure, his mind and his body, his education and his recreation, his love and his religion. He hardly knows which is which. He simply pursues his vision of excellence at whatever he does, leaving others to decide whether he is working or playing. To him he is always doing both."

~Lawrence Pearsall Jacks

"The moment at hand is the only thing we really own."

That lesson comes from a John Denver song, "On the Wings of a Dream."

Indeed, that's all we truly own, is the moment we are living in right now. Our lives are shaped by the moments we live. And right now, at this very moment, you have it within you to shape how you want the moment to unfold.

Every moment you shape, you create your life.

The nice, safe comfort zone doesn't do much to make the heart come alive. Once you've settled into a routine, you've traded passion for mediocrity. When was the last time you were completely challenged by something that you've never done before?

When you step back from your life and look at it from a completely different angle, you can't help but to learn from this new perspective.

So how do you begin walking on the edge of life again?

Do something new with a beginner's mind.

Put aside all your previous knowledge, expectations, and judgments.

Start fresh. Go passionately in the direction that your heart is calling you in.

It's simple, really.

What matters?

What's truly important?

Live your life by meaningful guidance.

Ask yourself:

Will this matter ten minutes,

ten months,

or ten years from now?

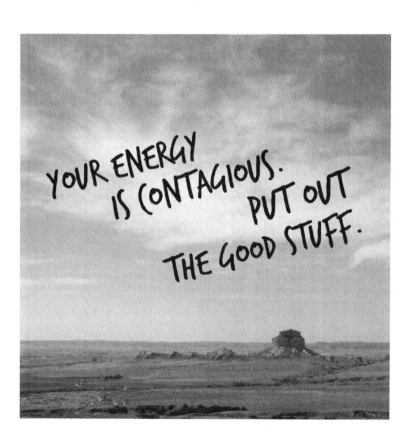

Have you ever been around someone with energy so vibrant you just want to hang with them for hours?

Energy is contagious.

The energy you have within you radiates outward.

You can choose this energy by your thoughts, your attitudes, and your actions.

Put out the good stuff.

SOMETIMES
THE BEAUTY
IS RIGHT NEXT
TO YOU,
BUT
YOU MISS
IT BECAUSE
YOU'RE LOOKING FOR
SOMETHING
FURTHER AWAY.

"Sometimes the beauty is right next to you,

but you miss it because you're looking for something further away."

~Patrick Wehner

We want. We want. Want more. And more.

We keep looking, search, longing.

And in that search, we sometimes miss the beauty that was right there all along.

TAKE
CHANCES.
MESS UP.
DO OVER.
YUP,
YOU GOT
THIS.

Feeling stuck?

Does one day blend into the next?

It's time for a change.

For you to stretch the boundaries of who you are, you must do things you've never done before.

Take action in a new direction.

IF YOU WANT
    YOUR LIFE
       TO BE AN
         AMAZING
       STORY,
        START
    LIVING
       IT.

How do you want your life story to read?

If you're not crazy about your past, now is the perfect time to start in a **new direction** to create the amazing story you want your life to be.

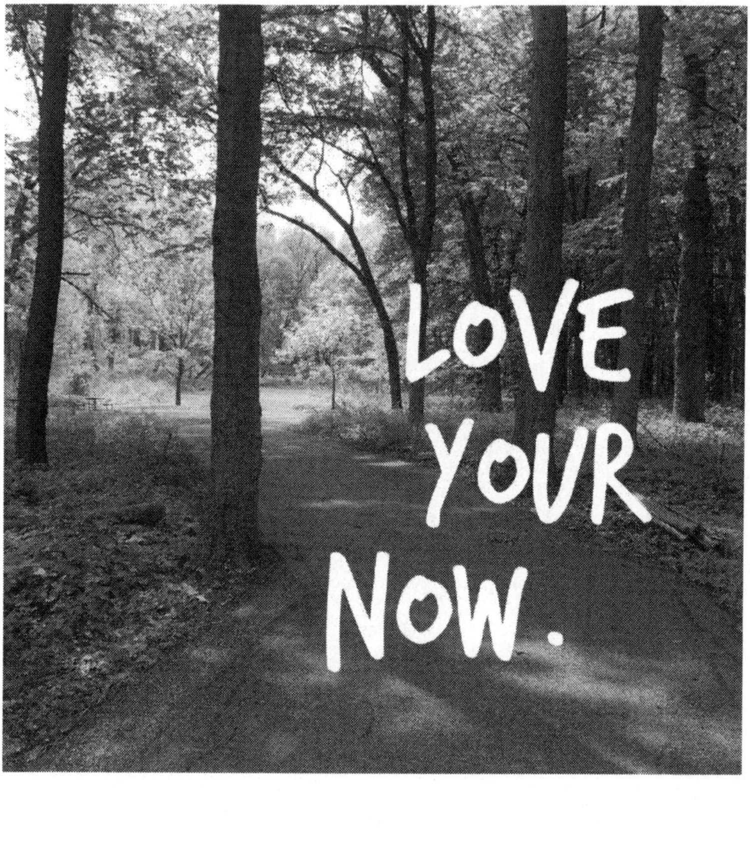
LOVE
YOUR
NOW.

Stop for a minute.

Close your eyes.

Breathe.

Repeat.

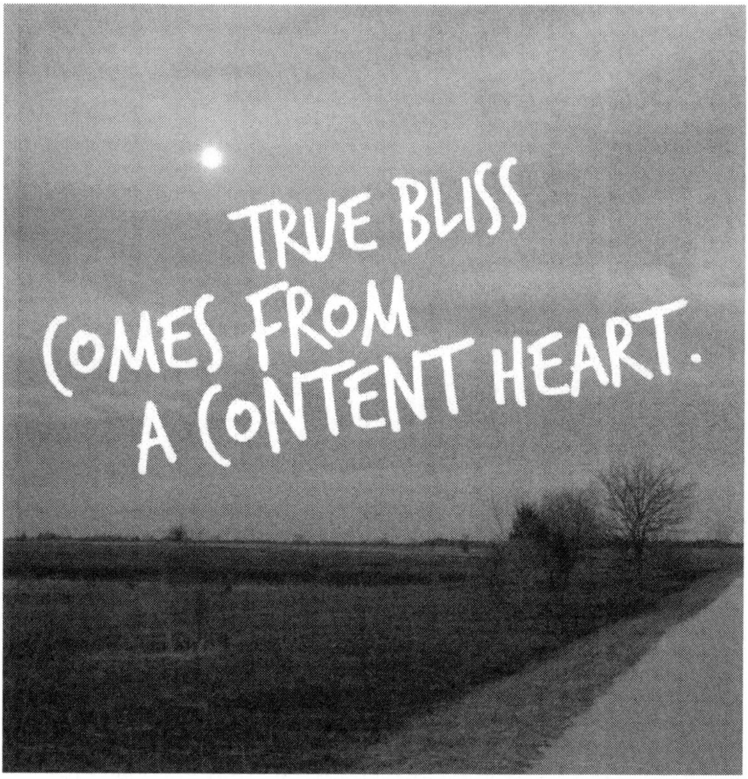
TRUE BLISS
COMES FROM
A CONTENT HEART.

Bliss is an interesting word.

It means "extreme happiness" or "ecstasy."

I prefer to see it as "quiet contentment."

Bliss is that state of mind when the moment you're experiencing is complete.

You are content.

You are grateful.

You are peaceful.

Bliss.

EVERY PATH HAS
A LESSON.

Some of the hardest lessons in life have turned out to be blessings in disguise. Every path on your life journey has a lesson embedded within it.

If you are going down a path that is wrong for you, branch off into a new direction.

Create a new path.

Find a new buddy to take the journey with you.

Most of all, look for the lesson.

And learn from it.

When there is struggle,

you'll often find a closed mind.

Open your heart.

You will find that your mind
opens, too.

WHEN WE PURSUE
THINGS IN
LIFE THAT ARE
SIGNIFICANT,
THAT REALLY
MATTER,
WE HAVE JOY.

You can invite **joy** into your life by pursuing things that truly matter to you.

Say "no" to things that rob you of your valuable time.

Fear and worry are two things that take the fun out of living. Every minute that you spend in fear and worry robs you of the present moment.

Don't give away your

precious time

to something that steals your life away in bits and pieces.

What kind of life do you want to have?

Every decision you make creates the life you're living.

If you are not happy about the life you have right now,

you must make different decisions.

Lost?

Sometimes the only way to find yourself is to get off the path you're on and take a new one.

Doubt is the thief of life.

Every accomplishment begins with a belief.

You must see yourself living the life you want.

You must see yourself doing the things you dream of.

You must believe.

YOU
NEVER KNOW WHEN
SOME WORDS
OF ENCOURAGEMENT,
A KINDNESS,
OR A HUG
CAN CHANGE
SOMEONE'S DAY.
REACH OUT.

Having a tough moment in your day?

Someone else probably is, too.

Reach out.

Bless someone with words of encouragement,

a kindness, or a hug.

It's a surefire way to turn around your own rough spot.

Life becomes an exciting adventure when you **open your heart** to new opportunities and discoveries.

Go in the direction of something new.

What you focus on in life, expands. This is not some hocus-pocus, flowery sentiment—it's based on the law of physics. What you put your attention on, expands. Shape new dreams in your mind by focusing on the vision you want to bring into your life.

You want **joy**?

Happiness?

Bliss?

What does that look like to you?

Focus on that.

Do you want to get to know yourself better?

Spend some time alone...

With you.

There's power in the pivot.

A pivot is a step in a totally new direction.

Even when you feel completely stuck--

You have the power to start over in a new direction...

Anytime.

If you live with limits, you'll never know the **possibilities.**

To live fully, you must test the boundaries of everything you can do.

If you're looking elsewhere for the **secret to happiness**, you'll never find it.

If you look within, it is there.

PASSION
IS CONTAGIOUS.
HANG AROUND
PEOPLE WHO ARE
LIVING
PASSIONATE
LIVES.

You want a life that's passionately full?

Go find people who are doing the things you want to do, living the life you want to live, achieving the things you want to accomplish.

You've probably heard the saying, "You're the sum of the five people you hang around most."

Passion is contagious.

It's also a two-way street. You'll attract passionate people into your life...if, and only IF, you are passionately engaged in life yourself.

If you're constantly stuck in the past or frequently thinking about the future, you're going to miss the beauty of today.

To be present in the moment requires you to embrace the experience of **NOW** in its entirety.

PASSION
IS WHAT
CARRIES
YOU
THROUGH
THE
TOUGHER
MOMENTS
OF LIFE.

If you have **passion** in your life—that fire in the belly, that defined purpose, that willingness to suffer for what you love—it will carry you through all the ups and downs of life.

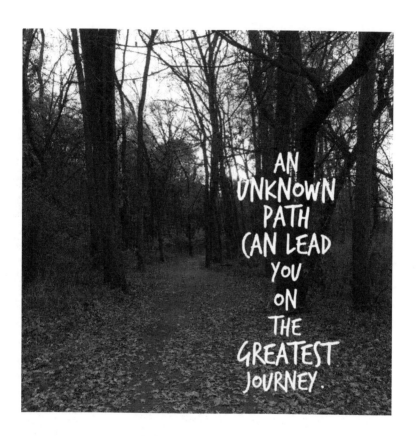

Life lies before us with lots of unknowns.

Some of the **greatest points on our journey** are centered in the unknown.

Kindness is energy.

It's a thought process.

It's an attitude.

It's a way of life.

It doesn't have to cost
a penny to be kind.

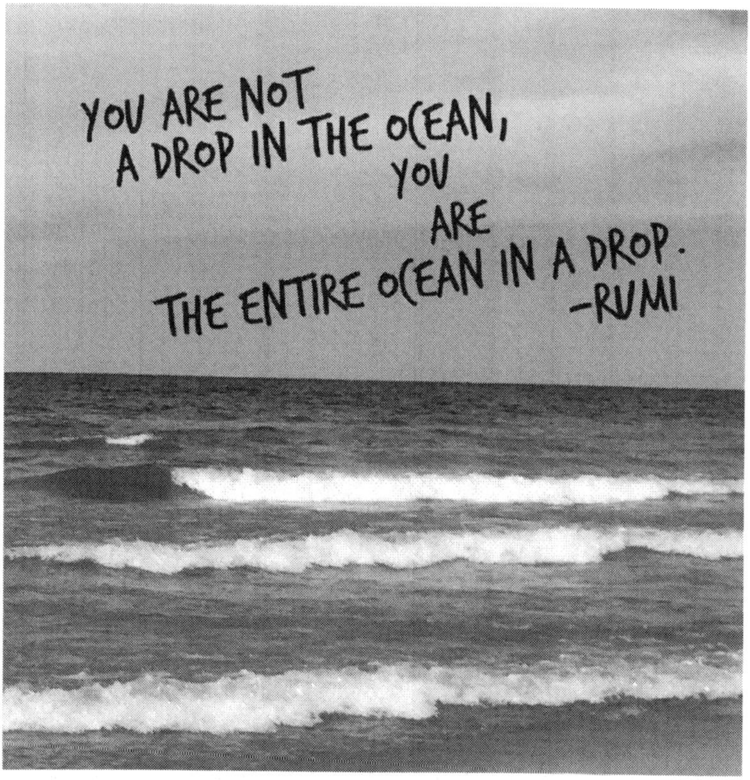
YOU ARE NOT
A DROP IN THE OCEAN,
YOU
ARE
THE ENTIRE OCEAN IN A DROP.
-RUMI

You matter.

It's as simple as that.

That rut you're stuck in?

Time to shake it up.

If you don't know what you're passionate about,

it's time to do something new.

Something that you've never done before—even if it's way out of your comfort zone.

ESPECIALLY if it's way out of your comfort zone.

What is it you've always wanted to try?

What are you curious about?

What do you imagine yourself doing?

Go bring something new into your life.

Live passionately.

Yup.

Just that.

It's a choice.

Go choose it.

What will people think?

If you live your life by that standard, you're not really living.

Be you.

People are going to judge anyway.

Need a do over?

Hit the reset button on life.

Yes, you can do that.

Start over with a fresh perspective and a new direction.

You are not your past.

The past does not define you.

Don't gamble the time you have today with the idea that you'll have enough time to do what you want later.

Tomorrow

is not promised.

"We had joy, we had fun, we had seasons in the sun, but the stars we could reach were just starfish on the beach."

~Terry Jacks, Seasons in the Sun

Life is full of seasons. Recognize when one season is ending and another is beginning. Seasons ebb and flow—so does life.

What calls to you?

What is the thing you MUST do?

What is your purpose?

The why of what you do?

That which your **soul** calls for—
that is the map of life.

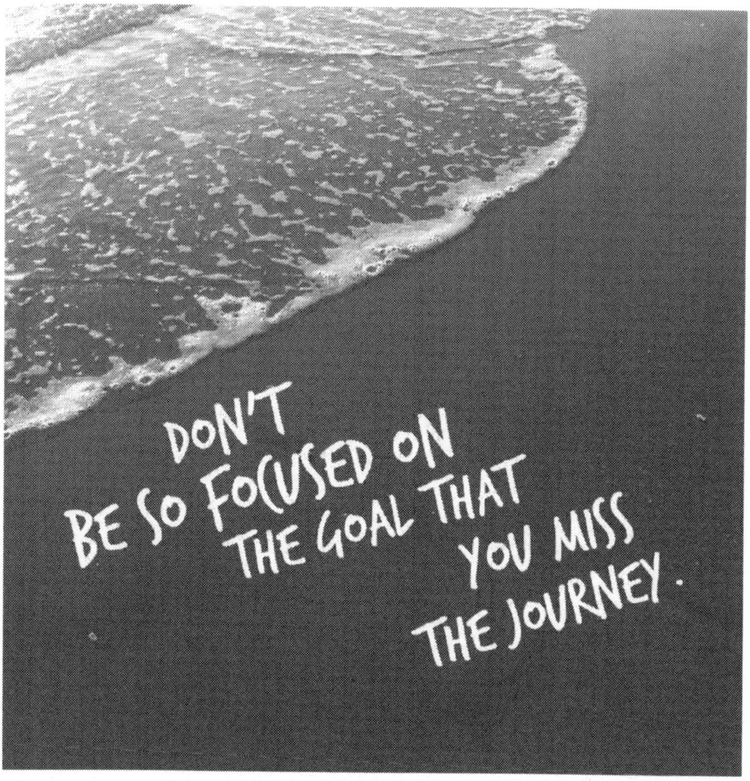
DON'T
BE SO FOCUSED ON
THE GOAL THAT
YOU MISS
THE JOURNEY.

If you are so deeply engrossed in chasing a goal,

you might miss the

journey called life.

ONLY THOSE WHO RISK
GOING FAR
WILL EVER
KNOW HOW JUST HOW
FAR THEY CAN GO.

What are the limits?

The boundaries?

The walls?

We don't know...

until we risk going too far.

WHEN
YOU STEP INTO
YOUR
AUTHENTICITY,
THERE ARE NO
BOUNDARIES
TO WHAT YOU
CAN DO.

There is no one who can do what you do, in the way that you do it.

Stay true to this.

Step into everything that is authentic to **YOU.**

You were not meant to be a carbon-copy of anyone else. In this whole wide world,

there is no one like you.

You were not born to blend in,

fit in,

or fly under the radar.

You were born to **stand out**.

Step into your uniqueness.

When life becomes challenging, it's easy to give up.

Sometimes it is difficult to see a positive outcome.

No matter what you're going through right now, know this:

The most difficult times can lead to your greatest triumphs.

Persist.

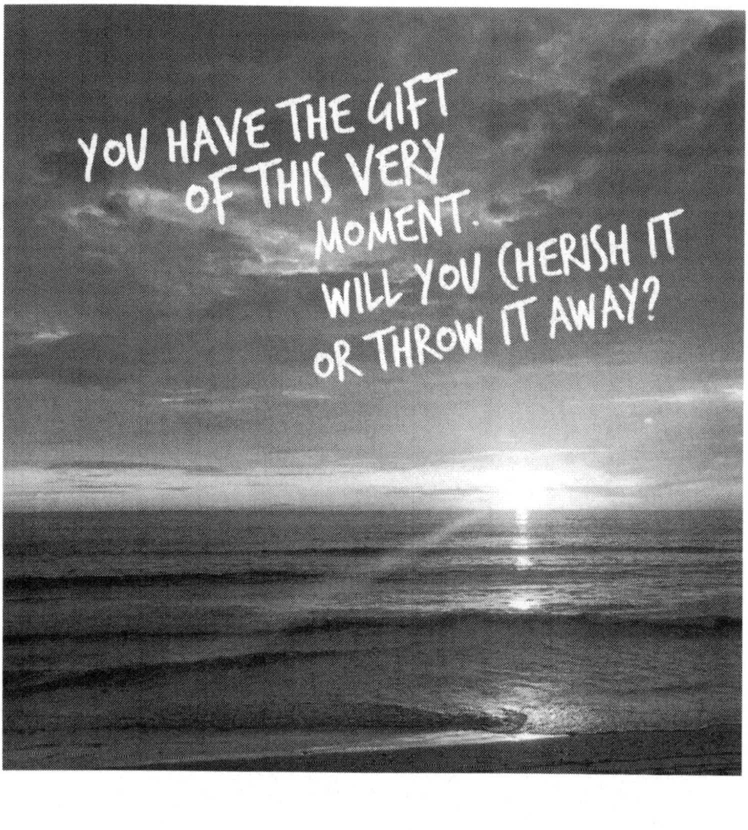
YOU HAVE THE GIFT
OF THIS VERY
MOMENT.
WILL YOU CHERISH IT
OR THROW IT AWAY?

Every moment is a gift.

It's up to you to cherish it
or throw it away.

Choose wisely.

Seek, and you shall find.

Look for the treasures—they're everywhere in life.

You might not notice them at first, but **look again**.

See everything from different angles--and you'll likely find the treasure was there all along.

THAT
DEEP-DOWN
ACHE IN
YOUR SOUL
IS TELLING
YOU
SOMETHING.

That longing for
something more,
something meaningful,
something **SIGNIFICANT**—
that's your soul speaking.

Listen.

PASSION IS THE BRIDGE TO JOY.

If you seek joy,

look for **passion.**

The bridge is there.

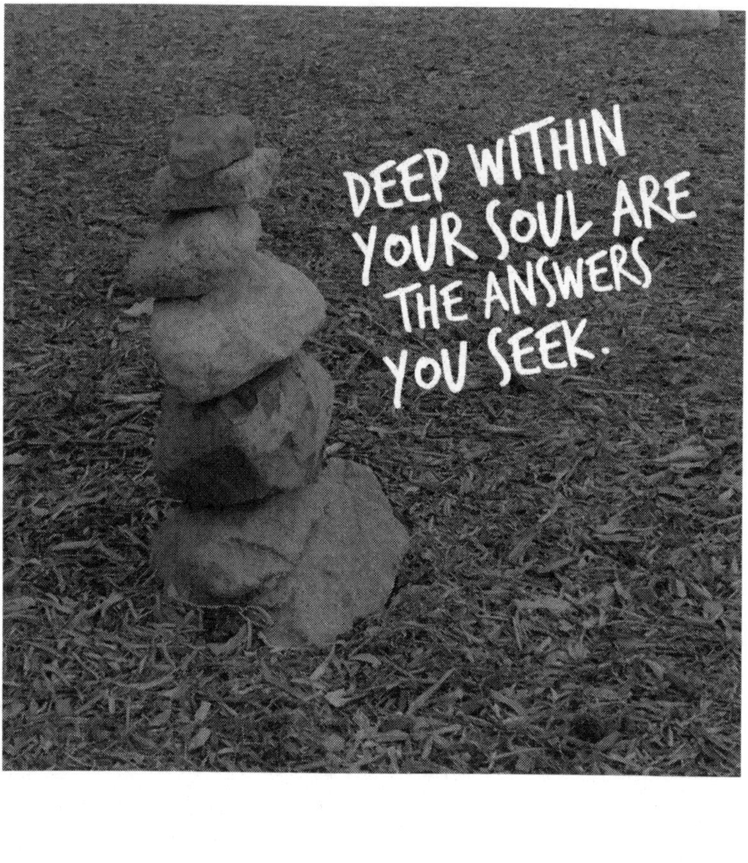
DEEP WITHIN
YOUR SOUL ARE
THE ANSWERS
YOU SEEK.

The answers to life?

They're deep within you.

Just another day for you...

It may be the last for someone else.

The ordinary day you're experiencing may be an extraordinary day for someone else.

Life is precious.

Don't waste an ordinary day.

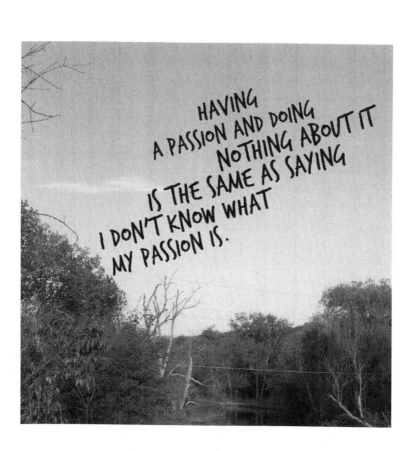

HAVING
A PASSION AND DOING
NOTHING ABOUT IT
IS THE SAME AS SAYING
I DON'T KNOW WHAT
MY PASSION IS.

Ignoring the passion that simmers within you and doing nothing about it is the same thing as saying "I have no idea what I'm passionate about."

The world needs your passionate energy.

Unwrap your passion.

Passion is the gift you've been given in life--with the purpose of sharing it with others.

In the crazy busyness of every day, it's all too easy to become lost in the million and one things

on your to-do list.

And it's all too easy to lose yourself in the process.

Be still.

Take time to set aside the craziness and embrace the stillness.

You'll find yourself there.

Every experience you have in life is a **gift.**

It may not seem like it at the time, but when you look for blessing in every situation, you'll find the lessons embedded in each one.

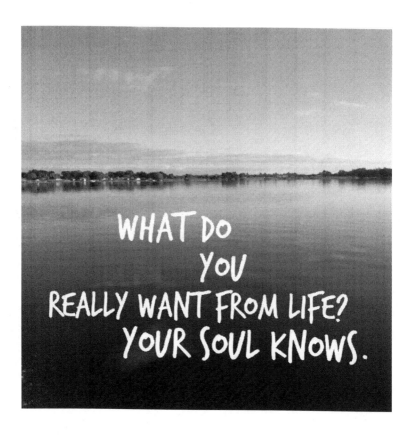

"I don't know what I want from life."

You know.

Search your soul.

Experience more.

Open your mind.

It's impossible to have an empty heart when you practice

gratitude.

Stop for a moment to think about the visions you have within you.

What do you dream of?

As Kody Bateman, owner of SendOutCards says:

"The stories in your mind become the stories of your life."

If the thoughts in your head are constantly filled with worry, anxiety, fear, and dread, that energy will become the story of your life. You can change that. The simplest, easiest way to do that is to shift your mindset to one of gratitude.

What are you grateful for?

What can you celebrate?

When you trudge through life the same way day after day, life becomes pretty one-dimensional.

Wayne Dyer said,

"When you change the way you look at things, the things you look at change."

Change your perspective and you'll get a whole new view on life.

Life is not one big goal to reach the end...

It's a **journey** to be embraced.

If there is no passion in the decision you're making, is it the right one for you?

Let **passion** guide you.

Thank you for being a part of this journey.

I hope you were blessed by the words in this book.

Karen Putz

www.agelesspassions.com

karen@agelesspassions.com